100 WAYS OF OVERCOMING PRESENTATION ANXIETY

DR DHEERAJ MEHROTRA

Contents

PREFACE

Public speaking is a prevalent anxiety for students, professionals, and even seasoned presenters. Presenting in a classroom, boardroom, or public setting can be terrifying. Fortunately, with the appropriate mindset, methods, and practice, presenting anxiety can be conquered.

This book, 100 Ways of Overcoming Presentation Anxiety, is a practical guide for anyone with stage fright, uneasiness, or lack of confidence when speaking in public. It uses proven methods, psychological insights, and real-life experiences to help readers build confidence, organise compelling presentations, and give powerful speeches without fear.

This book gives you 100 strong strategies to increase your confidence and make presentations easily, whether you're a student preparing for a school presentation, a professional doing a business pitch, or a leader addressing a vast crowd.

It is time to transform anxiety into sincerity, fear into focus, and uncertainty into confidence. Join me in being a brave, entertaining, and compelling speaker!

www.authordheerajmehrotra.com

I

100 Ways of Overcoming Presentation Anxiety

People who are compelled to speak in front of an audience frequently feel presentation anxiety. This is a regular sensation that many people experience. This book discusses various methods that can assist individuals in managing and overcoming their fears, enabling them to present confidently and clearly. If one practices these skills, nervous energy can be transformed into a powerful instrument for effective communication.

Understanding Presentation Anxiety

Presentation anxiety, often referred to as stage fright, can manifest in physical symptoms such as sweating, shaking, or a racing heart. It can also lead to mental blocks and self-doubt. Recognizing that this anxiety is a normal reaction can be the first step toward overcoming it. Let us learn more about how to over come the situation at ease.

1. Learn to take slow, deep breaths

In the moments leading up to your presentation, you find yourself backstage. Your palms began to sweat, and your heart began to speed. Inhale for four seconds, hold, then exhale for six seconds. Take slow, deep breaths. In this way, your nervous system is calmed. Just momentarily, see your breath as a wave that dissolves tension. Breathing deeply fills your brain with oxygen, which in turn helps you think more effectively. Focus on your breath rather than the audience as you take the stage. Using this straightforward method, you will feel more in control of the situation. Deep breathing can become a trustworthy strategy over time, allowing one to transform worry into composure instead.

2. Imagine yourself succeeding

You feel overwhelmed by "what ifs" the night before your presentation. Instead, you should close your eyes and see yourself succeeding in overcoming this overwhelming feeling. Imagine the audience smiling, nodding, and applauding what you just said. Feel the self-assurance in your posture and the way you speak. As a result of training your brain to anticipate success, visualisation can help reduce anxiety. Athletes utilise this method to prepare themselves for competitions; it is also effective for presentations. Building up your self-confidence can be accomplished by mentally practising a successful outcome. If the time comes, your mind will remember your envisioned success, making it much simpler to produce.

3. Take Baby Steps

Situation: You have a terrible fear of public speaking in front of huge groups of people. To get started, give a presentation to a small audience that is supportive, such as your family or friends. You should practise your speech in a setting with little to no pressure. You should gradually raise the size of the audience as your self-assurance rises. Consider presenting to a group of five people before addressing a group of fifty. You can develop your comfort zone by taking baby steps, making more extensive presentations less daunting. The more successes you have, the more confident you become in your talents. As time passes, you will see that the fear of beginning is frequently more severe than the actual event itself.

4. Learn Your Subject Matter

You will deliver an unfamiliar project, and the ambiguity is fuelling your worry. Investigate and comprehend your subject matter in great detail to combat this. Please make an effort to describe it using everyday language. When you completely understand the content, you have greater control. If you experience anxiety, your expertise will help you get through it. For example, if you present a sales report, you should practise the most critical elements until they appear natural. When you have confidence in your expertise, it is easier to overcome the anxiety of tripping or forgetting facts.

5. Please pay attention to the Message Itself, Not Yourself

Situation: You are concerned about how the audience will evaluate your performance. Make the worth of your message the focal point of your attention rather than yourself. Make sure you keep in mind that the audience is there to learn, not to criticise you. For instance, if you are presenting a new marketing plan, you should focus on how the organisation would gain from implementing the strategy. When you put the message ahead of your insecurities, you transform into a conduit for information rather than the focal point of attention. This frame of mind helps you connect with your audience and decreases the self-consciousness you experience.

6. Get there early

The situation is that you are in a hurry to get to the location, and the stress is making your anxiety worse. Make sure to arrive early to become acquainted with the area. Adjust the lighting, check the slides, and ensure the microphone works correctly. Walking along the stage beforehand will make you feel more in control of the situation. If you are presenting at a conference, for example, arriving early allows you to meet and greet people and establish a connection with them. You will feel more prepared and confident if you are familiar with the environment because it will be less surprising. This simple action can considerably alleviate the anxiety that comes before a presentation.

7. Use positive affirmations

You are having second thoughts about your capabilities just before a significant presentation. You can combat negative thoughts by repeating positive affirmations to yourself, such as "I am prepared," "I am confident," and "I can do this." You can say these phrases out loud or think them to yourself. As an illustration, if you present to top management, you should remind yourself of previous achievements. Your mind is rewired through affirmations, which replace fear with self-belief. This practice will, over time, lead to accumulating a reservoir of confidence that you can draw with whenever anxiety strikes.

8. In front of a mirror, you should practise.

Regarding your body language and facial emotions, you are uncertain about how you should behave. To *evaluate your performance, you should practise your presentation in front of a mirror. You should pay attention to your posture, gestures, and eye contact. For example, if you are about to give a proposal, train yourself to smile and remain open during the presentation. You may improve your delivery by using the mirror, which helps you become more conscious of how you come across to others. This self-awareness will increase your confidence, ensuring you appear poised and engaged throughout the presentation.*

9. Make a Self-Recording

While giving a presentation, you are unsure of how you appear or sound. During your practice, record yourself and then listen to the playback. Consider your body language, as well as your tone and tempo. If you are giving a significant address, for instance, recording it can assist you in identifying areas in which you could provide more improvement. When you see yourself succeeding, it also helps you create confidence. Using this method, you will receive helpful feedback, enabling you to improve your delivery and minimise your fear about how others may see you.

10. Divide it up into more manageable chunks

In this scenario, the idea of giving a presentation that lasts for thirty minutes is overwhelming to you. The task should be broken down into more manageable chunks. Take your time and concentrate on one section at a time, such as the introduction, the main points, and the verdict. For instance, you should approach each component individually if you are delivering a research report. By taking this technique, the task appears to be less intimidating. You can conquer one section at a time, allowing you to create momentum and confidence, ultimately making the presentation more straightforward to manage.

11. Get the audience involved early on

The situation is that you are becoming anxious about attracting the audience's attention. To quickly engage people, you should begin with a question, a narrative, or a poll. For instance, if you are introducing a new product, you could ask, "How many of you have had this problem? As a result of this engagement, the attention is shifted from you to the audience, which helps to calm your anxiety. The audience's early engagement also helps establish a relationship, making the remainder of the presentation more like a discussion than a performance.

12. Wear Comfortable Clothes

You are concerned that your attire will cause you to become distracted throughout the presentation. Opt for something that is both professional and comfy. For instance, if you are about to give a presentation at a conference, you should choose comfortable clothes that give you self-assurance. Steer clear of anything that is excessively snug or strange. This allows you to concentrate on your delivery rather than making adjustments to your clothes when you are physically comfortable. This seemingly insignificant aspect has the potential to alleviate anxiety dramatically.

13. Make intelligent use of your notes.

Situation: You are concerned that you will forget important details. To help you navigate, you should prepare brief notes or cue cards. You may, for instance, jot down bullet points for each segment of your presentation if you are presenting a complicated subject. Rather than reading the entire document word for word, utilise the annotations as prompts. Having a safety net helps you feel less anxious about blanking out, which in turn enables you to communicate in a more natural and self-assured manner.

13. Pay attention to the kind faces.

There is a situation in which you feel threatened by the crowd. Please find a few people in the throng who are friendlier than others and concentrate on them. For instance, if you are presenting to a large group, you should search for folks smiling or nodding their heads. A sense of connection and support is created as a result of this. Your confidence will increase, and you will experience less isolation if you concentrate on positive reactions.

15. Engage in mindful practices.

Anxious thoughts are consuming you to the point of becoming overwhelmed. Staying present at the moment is an essential part of practising mindfulness. For instance, when presenting a project, you should concentrate on your words and the audience's reactions rather than your concerns. Mindfulness helps you refrain from overthinking and maintain your composure. When it comes to relieving anxiety, specific techniques, such as practising mindful breathing or grounding exercises, might be particularly useful.

16. Perform a drill at the actual location.

Your anxiety is caused by being in a new environment. If possible, try to practise in the exact location. For instance, if you will give a presentation at a conference, you should go to the room before you start. Familiarizing yourself with the area makes you feel more in control and decreases the number of surprises you encounter. This practice also allows you to adjust to the layout and acoustics of the room, which will enhance your confidence.

17. Rely on Humour

Situation: You are concerned about giving the impression that you are stiff. Beginning with a humorous joke or tale is a great way to break the ice. For instance, you could give a presentation to your coworkers and tell them a story they can relate to. When you use humour, you humanise yourself and calm the audience, which in turn helps you feel more at ease. However, ensuring that your humour is acceptable and pertinent to the situation is essential.

18. Have Realistic Expectations

As a result of your fear of making mistakes, you are constantly striving for perfection. Remind yourself that there is no such thing as a perfect presentation.

For instance, when presenting a training session, you should concentrate on offering value rather than perfection. In addition to lowering the pressure you feel, setting reasonable expectations will help you approach the presentation with a more positive frame of mind.

19. Strike a Power Pose.

When you are about to take the stage., you may feel inadequacy and insecurity. To increase your self-assurance, maintain a power pose for two minutes with your hands on your hips and your chest open. This method can also be used if you are operating backstage; Power poses raise testosterone levels and lower cortisol levels, making you feel more confident and less apprehensive.

20. Put your attention on your capabilities.

Currently, you are having doubts about your capabilities. Bring to mind your accomplishments and the qualities that make you unique. For instance, if you are going to give a proposal, you should go back to cases in which your ideas were positively received. Concentrating on your strengths may boost your self-confidence and change your perspective from fear to capacity.

21. Perform drills using a timer.

The situation is that you are concerned about either finishing too quickly or going over the allotted time. Use a timer to practise your presentation to ensure you don't exceed the given time. As an illustration, if you are going to give a presentation that is ten minutes long, you should practise until you can deliver it when you are comfortable doing so. You may lessen the ambiguity and improve your delivery's velocity by timing yourself. Your self-assurance will increase, and you won't have to worry about falling behind at the last minute.

22. Make use of visual aids.

You are anxious about forgetting important details. To complement your presentation, you should use visual aids such as slides, charts, or videos. For example, a well-designed graph can help reinforce your message if you are elaborating on data. Visual aids can keep the audience interested and act as cues, alleviating the strain of recalling everything. Due to the planned flow they generate, your delivery will be less stressful and more fluid.

23. Pay Attention to What You Are Passionate About

You are presenting a topic that you are pretty enthusiastic about, but you are nevertheless experiencing feelings of anxiety. Ensure that your delivery reflects your level of enthusiasm. For instance, if you are talking about a project that you are very enthusiastic about, make sure that your enthusiasm is evident. Enthusiasm is infectious and has the potential to overshadow anxiety. By concentrating on why you are interested in the subject matter, the audience will be able to connect with your enthusiasm, making the presentation more engaging for everyone.

25. Become skilled at active listening.

You are concerned about the audience's response to the situation. Engage in active listening if participating in a question-and-answer session or a discussion. Whenever someone asks you a question, for instance, you should pay close attention and respond with some consideration. Getting involved with the audience helps to redirect attention away from your anxiety and onto the engagement. Additionally, active listening promotes the development of rapport, which results in the experience feeling more like a conversation than a performance.

26. Make use of a script for significant sections.

Consider the following scenario: you are concerned about forgetting vital details. Put together a screenplay for the most essential parts of the paper, such as the introduction or the conclusion. For instance, if you discuss a complicated concept, having a script will ensure you cover all the essential topics. Even if you do not have to commit it to memory word *for word, having a script provides a safety net that reduces the danger of forgetting what you are about to say.*

27. Take a stroll before the event.

Context: You are experiencing feelings of restlessness and anxiety in the lead-up to your presentation. Going for a brief stroll is a great way to let go of nervous energy and calm your mind. By way of illustration, if you are attending a conference, you should go outside for a few minutes. Endorphins are released, and stress hormones are decreased when you engage in physical activity, which in turn helps you feel calmer and more focused. When you go for a stroll, you give your mind a break, enabling you to return feeling renewed.

28. Make use of a checklist.

There is a situation in which you are concerned about missing something significant. Include everything you require, from slides to handouts, on your checklist. For instance, if you give a presentation at a conference, you should ensure that your materials are prepared the night before. Using a checklist, you can reduce the tension you experience at the last minute. Your confidence will increase, and you can concentrate on conveying your message when you know you have covered all the areas.

29. Do some drills with a friend.

Situation: You are uncertain about how people will react to your presentation. Put your skills to the test before a reliable friend or coworker and solicit their reactions. As an illustration, if you are getting ready to give a presentation at a job interview, you should practice with a mentor. You may improve your delivery by paying attention to constructive criticism and raising your confidence by receiving encouraging reinforcement. Another benefit of practising with someone is that it simulates an audience, making the event less daunting.

30. Pay Attention to the First Minute

Situation: You are feeling anxious about getting off to a good start. Focus on being an expert in the first minute of your presentation. As an illustration, if you are about to give a speech, you should practise your opening until it feels natural. The rest of the presentation will be much simpler if you get off to a solid start, which establishes the tone and develops momentum. You will eventually find your rhythm and feel more at ease once you have overcome the initial nerves that you received.

SHEAKER.
SHEAKING!

31. Use a method that helps you relax.

You are experiencing feelings of tension and being overpowered. Examine the effectiveness of a relaxing method such as progressive muscle relaxation. If you are backstage, for instance, you should first tension and then release each muscle group, beginning with your toes. Applying this method alleviates body tension, which helps relax the mind. The sensation of physical relaxation facilitates approaching the presentation with a more precise and focused mentality.

32. Be wary of Caffeine

You are feeling nervous and anxious in the lead-up to your presentation. Avoid caffeine, as it can make you feel even more worried. For instance, if you are giving a presentation in the morning, you should choose herbal tea over coffee. Consuming water regularly makes you feel more in control of your body. AReducingyour consumption of stimulants will help you maintain your composure and remain calm.

33. Employ a Narrative Method of Approach

There is a situation in which you are concerned about losing the audience's interest. Your presentation should be organised as a tale, with a prominent beginning, middle, and conclusion. For instance, if you are trying to sell a product, you should describe a problem, give your solution, and conclude with a success story. Sharing stories will make Your information more enjoyable and easier to read. In addition, it facilitates an emotional connection with the audience, which in turn helps you reduce your concentration on nervousness.

34. Attend to the way you carry yourself.

Currently, you are unsure of how to appear confident in a situation. Make an effort to cultivate open and positive body language by standing tall, maintaining eye contact, and utilising natural movements. For instance, if you are giving a presentation to a group of people, you should avoid crossing your arms or fidgeting. Not only does confident body language reassure the audience, but it also fools your brain into feeling more self-assured through body language.

35. Get ready to answer questions.

You are experiencing anxiety about the question and answer session. Prepare responses that are well thought out and anticipate any enquiries that may be asked. For instance, if you explain a new policy, you should consider the potential issues the audience might have beforehand. When you are well-prepared, you lessen the likelihood of getting caught off guard. In addition to this, it exhibits your competence, which improves your self-confidence.

36. Utilise a Mantra

If you cannot cope with the barrage of opposing ideas, recite a calming mantra, such as "I am calm and capable" or "This too shall pass." For instance, if you are waiting to present, you can silence yourself and repeat your mantra to bring yourself back to the centre. Mantras serve as a mental anchor, assisting you in maintaining your composure and concentration.

37. Gratitude should be practised.

You are experiencing anxiety because of the presentation. Gratitude is a practice that can help you shift your thinking. For instance, you should remind yourself of the possibility of having your team's support or the opportunity to share your knowledge. Concentrating on the positive aspects of a situation helps lessen worry. In addition, it enables you to see the presentation from a different perspective, making it feel less intimidating.

38. Making use of a structured outline

You are concerned that you might lose your line of thought; this is the situation. Develop an outline that is well-structured and contains distinct sections and transitions. For instance, if you submit a report, you should divide it into three sections: the introduction, the findings, and the suggestions. When you have a defined structure, you can stay on topic, and the risk of rambling or forgetting important points is reduced.

39. Have a grin

You may be anxious about giving the impression that you're overly tense. Always remember to smile, even if you don't feel like it. For instance, if you are standing in front of the audience and greeting them, a genuine grin will establish a favourable initial impression. When you smile, endorphins are released into your body, which helps you feel more relaxed and reduce stress. It also gives the impression that you are friendly and self-assured.

40. Take a look at the bigger picture.

You are becoming bogged down by the insignificant minutiae of the situation. Bring to mind the bigger picture, which is the reason why your presentation is essential. For instance, When pitching a concept, you should concentrate on its potential impact rather than its minor defects. By keeping the big picture in mind, you can limit your tendency towards perfectionism *and maintain your motivation.*

41. Honour even the little victories.

You may feel discouraged because of previous errors. However, you should rejoice in minor victories, such as finishing a practice run or receiving great comments. For instance, if you have improved the quality of your delivery, you should acknowledge your progress. Celebrating even the most minor victories generates momentum and strengthens your confidence, making the next step feel more attainable.

42. Make use of a routine for warming up.

In the moments before your presentation, you may experience stiffness and nervousness. To prepare, you should establish a routine for warming up, which may include stretching, singing, or tongue twisters. For instance, if you are giving a presentation in the morning, allocate five minutes to warming up your voice and body. This regimen will help you feel more physically prepared and relaxed, which will help you feel less anxious and significantly improve your delivery.

43. Attend to the Requirements of the Audience

If you are concerned about how people will view you in the future, focus on the audience's requirements and how your presentation might assist them. For instance, if you are giving a workshop, consider the skills that the attendees will acquire. Concentrating on the audience's requirements can calm your anxiety and make the presentation feel more purposeful and less about you.

44. Implement a Soothing Object

You are experiencing anxiety and need a tool to help you feel more grounded. Take a tiny comforting object, such as a smooth stone or jewellery. For instance, if you are going to give a presentation at a conference, you should keep the item in your pocket. In times of stress, a discreet touch might bring peace and stability to the person touching it.

45. Positive self-talk should be practised.

You may be doubting your capabilities. You can replace negative ideas with positive self-talk, such as saying things like "I am prepared" or "I can handle this." For instance, if you present to senior management, you should remind yourself of your specialised knowledge. Constructively talking to oneself helps boost confidence and lessen the influence of self-doubt.

46. Use an Opening That Is Structured

Suppose, in a situation, You are feeling anxious about getting off to a good start. You should start with a structured beginning, such as a narrative, a statistic, or a quote from someone. Take, for instance, the case where you deliver a sales pitch: begin with an unexpected fact. Providing the rest of the presentation is much simpler if you have a good introduction that captures attention and establishes a confident tone.

47. Notes should be taken during rehearsals.

The situation is that you are concerned about forgetting important details. The best way to identify areas that need work is to take notes throughout practice. For instance, jot down the areas that require additional clarification if you are practising a speech. Reviewing your notes improves your delivery and gives you a sense of being better prepared.

48. Make use of a scent that is calming.

You are experiencing an overwhelming level of anxiety. To relax, use a calming perfume, such as peppermint or lavender. If you are backstage, apply some essential oil to your wrists. Inhaling the scent can calm your nerves and bring your thoughts back to the centre.

49. Pay Attention to Your Breathing

As the lecture progresses, you may experience panic. Maintaining your composure requires you to concentrate on your breathing. For instance, if you are giving a speech, you should hold your breath and take a deep breath before each new point. Controlled breathing can also help you maintain a constant pace and reduce anxiety.

50. Put a visual anchor to use.

You are afraid of losing your concentration on the task at hand. To ground yourself, select a visual anchor, such as a point on the wall or a friendly face. If you are presenting in a vast space, concentrate on a point in the back of the room. This method will help you maintain your awareness and reduce distractions.

51. Get Experience in a Variety of Environments

There is a situation in which you are concerned about adjusting to the atmosphere of the presentation. Put your skills to the test in various environments, such as a park or a different room. For instance, if you will give a presentation at a conference, you should practise in a room with analogous acoustics. The ability to adapt and confidence are enhanced by familiarity with various contexts.

52. Put a Power Word to Use

Your current state of mind is one of insecurity. Select a powerful word, such as "confidence" or "strength," and repeat it to yourself hushedly. For example, you could use your power words to improve your spirits when presenting to a vast audience. This straightforward method helps you maintain concentration while reinforcing a pleasant frame of mind.

53. Take Note of Your Advancement

You are feeling disheartened because of your previous errors. Focus on how far you've come. For instance, if you have improved your ability to speak in front of an audience, remind yourself of your progress. Celebrating your progress boosts your self-confidence and encourages you to continue evolving.

54. Use a Closing That Is Structured

Your presentation is about to conclude, and you feel uncomfortable. Prepare a decisive conclusion, such as a quote that will stick in your mind or a call to action. As an illustration, if you present an idea, you should conclude with a convincing incentive to take action. There is a lasting impression that is left by an organised closure, and it guarantees that you finish with confidence.

55. Engage in Gratitude Practices Beforehand

The situation is that you are experiencing anxiety because of the presentation. Gratitude is a practice that should be practised. For instance, When presenting to your coworkers, you should express gratitude for their support. Being grateful helps you shift your emphasis from fear to optimism, reducing anxiety and improving your psychological state.

56. Utilise a Timer to Take Breaks

You are concerned that you will not have enough time to complete the task. When you are giving your *presentation, you should arrange breaks using a timer. For instance, you should schedule brief breaks if you are leading a lengthy session. Breaks allow you to regain your composure and keep your energy levels up, making the presentation more bearable.*

57. Take Note of Your Voice

Think of a Situation: You are anxious about how you come across to others. To improve your clarity and impact, you should practise modulating your voice. When presenting statistics, for instance, you should change your tone to emphasise the most critical points. You can improve your delivery and feel less self-conscious with a voice that exudes self-assurance.

58. Utilise a question-and-answer format:

In this scenario, you are worried about being unable to respond to enquiries. To organise your question and answer session, repeat the question and pause before responding. By way of illustration, if you will be presenting a proposal, you should use this method to collect your thoughts. Using an organised strategy helps prevent panic and ensures that reactions are considered.

59. Engage in daily visualisation exercises.

You had been experiencing feelings of anxiety for several weeks before the presentation. Visualisation should be done daily to help create confidence. Imagine yourself being successful daily, for instance, if you are getting ready to give a keynote address. Visualisation in a consistent manner helps to reinforce a good mindset and minimises anxiety over the long run.

59. *Use a playlist that is relaxing.*

You may be experiencing anxiety in preparation for your presentation. To soothe your anxiety, listen to peaceful music. For instance, you may play some relaxing music backstage to help you get your bearings. If you listen to music, you will feel less stressed and be able to approach the presentation with a clear head.

60. *Pay Attention to Your Position*

Currently, you are unsure of how to appear confident in a situation. Maintaining proper posture by standing tall and keeping your shoulders back is important. For instance, if you are presenting in front of a group, you should keep an open position. Not only does adopting a confident stance reassure the audience, but it also helps you feel better about yourself.

61. Use a Schedule That Is Structured

You are concerned about getting lost. At the beginning of the meeting, introduce the audience to an organised agenda. For instance, you should summarise the most critical themes when leading a workshop. A clear agenda can help reduce nervousness by reassuring the audience and keeping you on track.

62. Exercise Your Skills in Front of a Camera

The situation is that you are unclear about how you appear to others. Watch the video of yourself giving a presentation that you recorded. For instance, if you are preparing to give a virtual presentation, you should practise in front of the camera. Monitoring your performance enables you to recognise areas where you could improve and boosts your confidence in your delivery.

63. Use an Object That Is Grounding

Currently, you are experiencing feelings of disconnection and anxiety. Throughout the presentation, you should keep a grounding object in your hand, such as a pen or a water bottle. While giving a presentation in a meeting, you should keep the object on the table. Simply touching it discretely can give the impression of steadiness.

64. Take Note of Your Influence

Currently, you are experiencing anxiety regarding the response of the audience. Concentrate on the positive effects that your presentation will have. For example, when discussing a fresh concept, you should consider how it can benefit others. Your perspective will transition from one of dread to one of purpose when you focus on effect.

65. Use a Story That Is Structured

You are concerned about keeping the audience interested. Your presentation should be organised like a tale, with a prominent beginning, middle, and conclusion. If you are presenting a case study, for instance, you should frame it as a narrative. Storytelling makes your content more approachable and more uncomplicated to comprehend.

66. Obtain Experience in Low-Pressure Environments

The situation is that you are anxious about giving presentations with big stakes. Experiment in low-pressure environments, such as community groups or informal get-togethers, for some practice. For instance, if you are getting ready to present at a conference, put on a presentation at a local event first. When performing in front of larger audiences, low-pressure rehearsal helps increase confidence and minimises nervousness.

67. Use a Phrase That Is Calming

You are experiencing feelings of being overcommitted. To bring oneself back to the centre, you should repeat a calming phrase, such as "I am calm and in control." For instance, if you are waiting to present, you should say the statement silently. Calming phrases offer mental reassurance and assist you in maintaining your composure.

68. Pay Attention to Your Preparation in

You have some reservations about your level of preparedness. Remind yourself of the time and work you have invested in getting ready. It is essential to have faith in your preparation, for instance, if you have practised several times. Putting your attention on the effort you put in will help you feel more confident and lessen feelings of self-doubt.

69. Use a Handout That Is Structured

The situation is that you are concerned about forgetting specifics. Make available a handout that is organised and contains the most important topics. As an illustration, the handout can be utilised as a reference if you are presenting a complicated subject. Keeping the audience interested and reducing the strain you feel when recalling everything is accomplished through this.

70. Conduct mindful breathing exercises.

You may be experiencing panic right now. A mindful breathing practice involves concentrating on each inhale and exhale. For instance, if you are addressing a large audience, carefully breathe before beginning your presentation. This approach helps you remain present while also calming your mind.

71. Utilise an Introduction That Is Structured

In this scenario, you are anxious about getting started. Create an organised introduction, such as a quick bio or a summary of the agenda, and start with that. For example, if you are presenting to prospective customers, you should introduce yourself and explain the reason for the meeting. A precise introduction establishes a confident tone.

72. Put your attention on your capabilities.

Currently, you are having doubts about your capabilities. Bring to mind your accomplishments and the qualities that make you unique. For instance, if you give a proposal, you should return to cases where your ideas were positively received. Building confidence and shifting your perspective from fear to capacity can be accomplished by concentrating on your strengths.

73. Utilise a Conclusion That Is Structured

Situation: You are concerned about concluding feebly. Planning a structured conclusion, such as a summary or a call to action, is essential. For instance, if you are trying to sell a product, you should conclude with a persuasive reason to purchase it. A powerful conclusion produces an impact that lasts and ensures that you finish with self-assurance.

74. Afterwards, Put Gratitude Into Practice

You are experiencing a sense of relief, but you are also concerned about giving comments. To show appreciation for finishing the talk, practise thankfulness. One example would be to express gratitude to the team for their attention after you have presented to them. Gratitude helps you shift your emphasis from dread to appreciation, reducing your anxiety after a presentation.

75. Making use of a structured outline

You are concerned that you might lose your line of thought; this is the situation. Develop an outline that is well-structured and contains distinct sections and transitions. For instance, if you submit a report, you should divide it into three sections: the introduction, the findings, and the suggestions. You can stay on target and reduce the risk of rambling if you have a clear structure.

76. Pay Attention to Your Breathing

As the lecture progresses, you find yourself experiencing feelings of panic. Maintaining your composure requires you to concentrate on your breathing. For instance, if you will give a speech, you should hold your breath and take a deep breath before each new point. Maintaining a constant pace and reducing anxiety are benefits of practising controlled breathing.

77. Put a visual anchor to use.

You are fearful of losing your concentration on the task at hand. To ground yourself, select a visual anchor, such as a point on the wall or a friendly face. Concentrate on a point in the back of the room, for instance, if you are presenting in a vast space. By using this method, you will be able to maintain your awareness and reduce distractions.

78. Get Experience in a Variety of Environments

There is a situation in which you are concerned about adjusting to the atmosphere of the presentation. Put your skills to the test in various environments, such as a park or a different room. For instance, if you will give a presentation at a conference, you should practise in a room with analogous acoustics. The ability to adapt and confidence are enhanced by familiarity with various contexts.

79. Put a Power Word to Use

Your current state of mind is one of insecurity. Select a powerful word, such as "confidence" or "strength," and repeat it to yourself hushedly. For example, you could use your power words to improve your spirits when presenting to a vast audience. This straightforward method helps you maintain concentration while reinforcing a pleasant frame of mind.

80. Take Note of Your Advancement

You are feeling disheartened because of your previous errors. Focus on how far you've come. For instance, if you have improved your ability to speak in front of an audience, remind yourself of your progress. Celebrating your progress boosts your self-confidence and encourages you to continue evolving.

81. Make use of a ritual before the presentation.

As you prepare for your presentation, you are experiencing feelings of disarray. Put together a pre-presentation routine that includes activities such as listening to a song you enjoy or performing a little stretch. For instance, if you are about to give a presentation at a conference, you should give yourself five minutes to gather your thoughts. A routine sends a message to your brain that it is time to concentrate, which helps you feel less anxious and more prepared for whatever comes your way.

82. Instead of focusing on perfection, pay attention to the process.

Suppose you are attempting to give an immaculate presentation but are afraid of making mistakes. Move your attention to the method, which entails conveying your message in a way that is both clear and genuine. For instance, you should emphasize engagement rather than perfection when giving a workshop. Embracing the process helps you connect with the audience and minimises the pressure you are under.

83. Use a Pause That Is Structured

The situation is that you are anxious about speaking faster than necessary. Incorporate predetermined pauses into your routine to slow down and collect your things. When presenting data, for instance, it is essential to pause after significant points to allow the information to sink in fully. Pauses also provide you with the opportunity to breathe, which helps to alleviate anxiety and improves clarity.

84. Exercise in the presence of a pet.

Given your current situation, practising in front of others may be difficult. Instead, conduct your rehearsals before a plush animal or a pet. For instance, if you are getting ready to give a speech, your dog can serve as an audience that does not pass judgment. This low-pressure practice can help you develop self-assurance and improve your delivery.

86. Make Use of a Form for Structured Feedback

Predicament: You are unaware of how to make improvements. Make use of a form that contains particular questions to request organised feedback. For instance, if you are giving a presentation to a group, you should enquire about your clarity, pace, and involvement. Constructive feedback helps you find areas in which you excel and those in which you could improve, boosting your confidence.

87. Pay Attention to Your Energy

You are experiencing exhaustion and anxiety. To boost your energy, take a short stroll, have a nutritious snack, or strike a power pose. Suppose your presentation is scheduled for the afternoon; a vigorous walk before it is a good idea. You feel more aware and confident throughout the day when you have more energy.

88. Employ an Icebreaker That Is Structured

You are experiencing anxiety over the prospect of engaging the audience. An organised icebreaker, such as a quick poll or a humorous fact, is a good place to begin this activity. Asking the question, "How many of you have worked here for more than a year?" is a good example to ask when presenting to a new staff." Icebreakers are a great way to calm your worries and create a relaxed atmosphere.

89. Make use of gestures when practising in front of a mirror.

The circumstance is that you are uncertain about your body language. Perform your exercises in front of a mirror, incorporating natural gestures. For instance, you should use hand movements to emphasise the most critical parts when presenting a proposal. Your delivery can be improved with mirror practice, and you will appear more assured.

90. Employ a Transition That Is Structured

You are concerned about stopping your flow. Organise transitions between sections in a structured manner. Clear transitions help keep your presentation organised and eliminate the worry of tripping. For instance, if you deliver a report, you should use sentences like "Now, let's move to the next point."

91. Make Use of a Schedule for Structured Rehearsal

You are feeling overburdened by the preparation. Develop a well-organised rehearsal schedule with a list of clear objectives for each session. For instance, if you are getting ready to deliver a keynote address, you should devote one session to the opening and another to the closing. Having a schedule helps ensure you are well prepared and eliminates stress at the last minute.

92. Train in a variety of different outfits.

Situation: You are uncertain about the appropriate clothes for your presentation. Experiment with various types of clothing to see which feels most professional and comfortable. During rehearsals, for instance, you should test your costume if you will be giving a presentation at a conference. Having a sense of self-assurance and reducing distractions are benefits of feeling secure in your clothing.

93. Use a Preparation for Structured Questions and Answers

In this scenario, you are worried about being unable to respond to enquiries. Prepare for the question and answer session by listing possible questions and practising your answers. For instance, if introducing a new policy, you should anticipate questions about its execution. When you are well-prepared, you lessen the likelihood of getting caught off guard.

94. Be mindful of your tone.

In this scenario, you are concerned about coming across as monotonous. Experiment with different tones to emphasise the most essential ideas. For instance, if you deliver a narrative, you should employ a lively tone for the thrilling portions and a serious tone for the vital elements. The audience is engaged, and self-consciousness is reduced when the speaker has a vibrant voice.

95. A structured closing question should be used.

Situation: You are anxious about concluding feebly. The concluding question was a structured inquiry, such as "What are your thoughts? ". or "What are some ways we can proceed?" As an illustration, if you present a concept, you should conclude by requesting input. In addition to ensuring a firm conclusion, a concluding question encourages participation.

96. Perform drills in front of a group that is encouraging.

In this situation, you feel uneasy when you are practising by yourself. Rehearse in front of a small group of people who are encouraging. As an illustration, if you are getting ready to give a presentation, you may invite your friends or coworkers to listen to you. Receiving constructive criticism helps you improve your delivery while also boosting your confidence.

97. Utilise a Visual Plan That Is Structured

Context: You are concerned about the presentations you have prepared. Make a structured visual layout, ensuring each slide supports the idea you want to convey. For instance, use straightforward charts and a minimum amount of text when presenting data. Your presentation will be improved, and your anxiety about technological issues will be reduced if you have a well-designed visual strategy.

98. Pay Attention to Your Pace

Anxiety arises because you are concerned about speaking too quickly or too slowly. It is essential to practise keeping a steady pace. For instance, if you are about to give a speech, you should time yourself to ensure you are not rushing through it. Maintaining a steady tempo makes you appear more assured and keeps the audience interested.

99. Make use of a structured question to warm up.

In this scenario, you are anxious about getting started. To get the audience interested and involved, begin with a warm-up question. For instance, if you are introducing a new product, you could ask, "How many of you have had this problem?" A warm-up question *helps break the ice and calms your worries.*

100. Gratitude for Your Achievements

Although you have finished the presentation, you continue to experience feelings of anxiety. Please spend some time celebrating your accomplishments, no matter how minor. One example would be rewarding yourself with something you enjoy doing after giving a presentation to a large audience. Celebrating helps to perpetuate pleasant thoughts and increases confidence for future presentations.

II

Pictorial Learning of Overcoming Presentation Anxiety

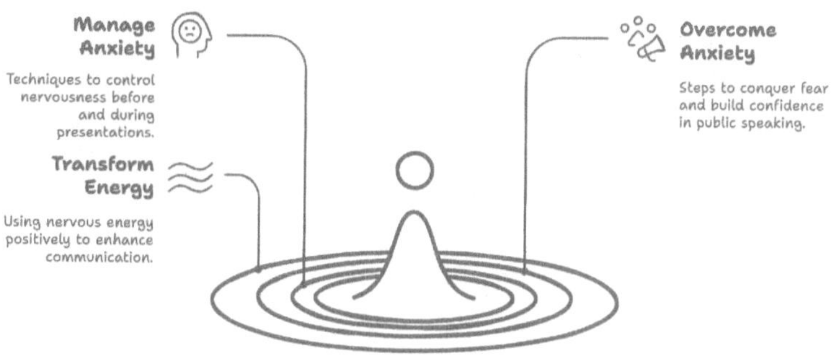

Transforming Anxiety into Growth

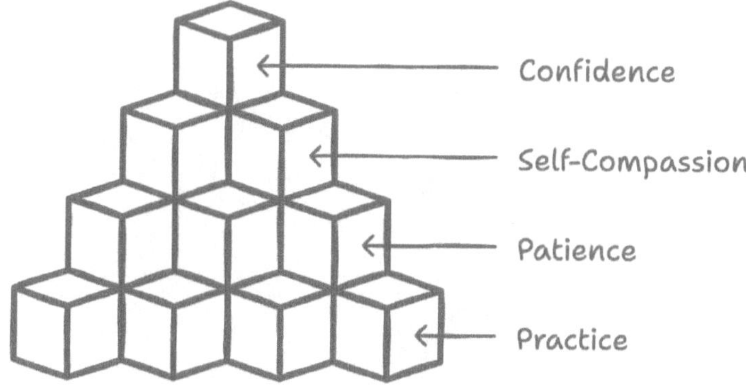

Overcoming Presentation Anxiety

Overcoming Presentation Anxiety

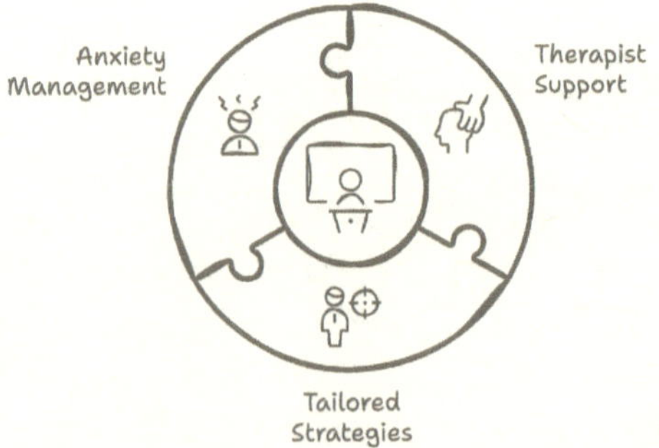

Overcoming Presentation Anxiety

How to effectively use visual aids in presentations?

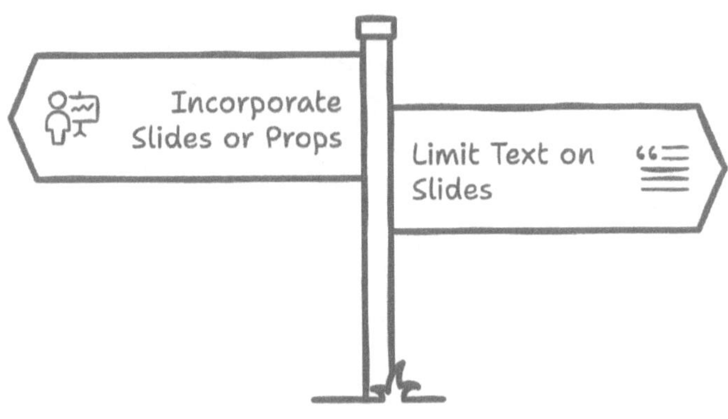

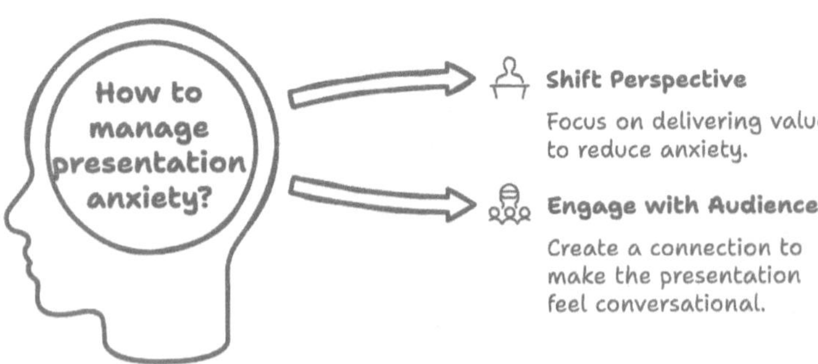

Relaxation Techniques Cycle

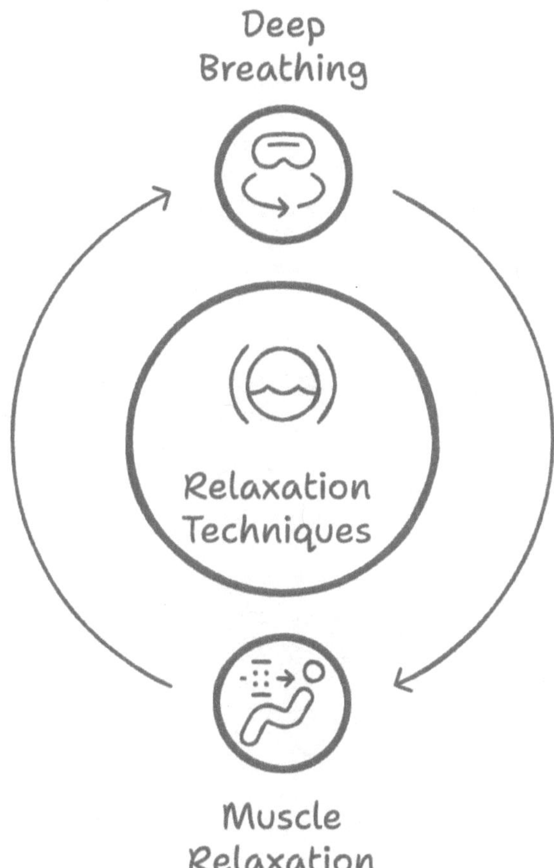

Steps to Overcome Presentation Anxiety

Organize Content

Structure presentation logically for clarity.

Practice

Rehearse multiple times to refine delivery.

Know Your Material

Familiarize yourself with the content to boost confidence.

Techniques for Confidence

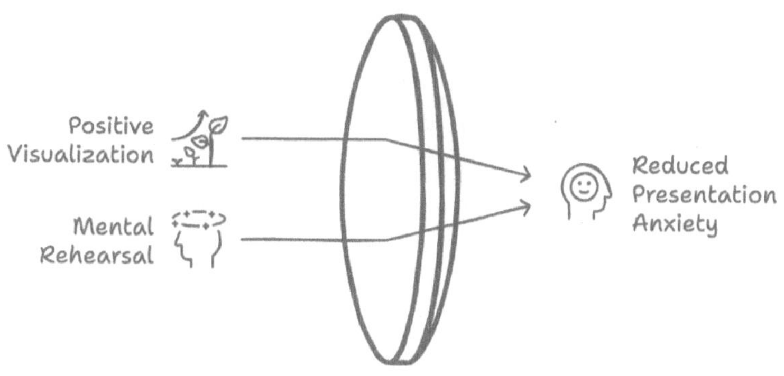

Understanding the Roots of Presentation Anxiety

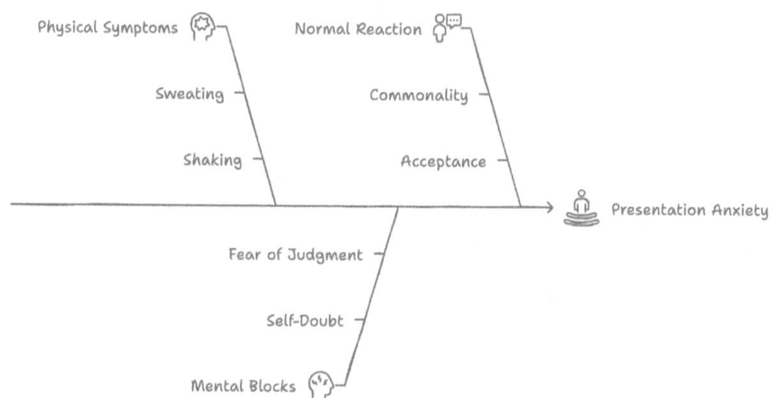

www.authordheerajmehrotra.com

Dr Dheeraj Mehrotra is a distinguished educational leader and innovator with over three decades of experience transforming education through excellence and innovation. A recipient of the President of India's National Teacher Award (2006), he is a certified expert in Six Sigma (White and Yellow Belt), Neuro-Linguistic Programming (NLP), and Total Quality Management (TQM). His specialisation encompasses academic audits, school quality assurance and accreditation (SQAA), and implementing Kaizen and 5S in schools. As an accomplished author, Dr. Mehrotra has published over 200 books on various subjects, including computer science, artificial intelligence, digital body language, quality circles, and school management. His contributions also include the development of more than 150 free educational mobile apps for teachers, students, and parents, a feat recognised by the Limca Book of Records and the India Book of Records. Dr. Mehrotra has served as Principal at prestigious institutions such as De Indian Public School in New Delhi, NPS International School in Guwahati, and Kunwar's Global School in Lucknow. He has also held the position of Education Officer at GEMS in Gurgaon, making significant contributions to the global education community. As a premier UDEMY instructor, Dr. Mehrotra has created over 500 courses that have impacted more than 800,000 learners across 180 countries. Additionally, as the founder and president of the IoT Society of India, he advocates for technology integration in education worldwide.

BOOKS BY THE SAME AUTHOR